Amazing Orbs

Orbs and Other Light Anomalies

PAM RAWORTH

To Maria
love & blessings
Pam xx

Balboa Press books may be ordered through booksellers or by contacting:

Balboa Press
A Division of Hay House
1663 Liberty Drive
Bloomington, IN 47403
www.balboapress.com
1-(877) 407-4847

Because of the dynamic nature of the Internet, any web addresses or links contained in this book may have changed since publication and may no longer be valid. The views expressed in this work are solely those of the author and do not necessarily reflect the views of the publisher, and the publisher hereby disclaims any responsibility for them.

Any people depicted in stock imagery provided by Thinkstock are models, and such images are being used for illustrative purposes only. Certain stock imagery © Thinkstock.

ISBN: 978-1-4525-8397-6 (sc)
ISBN: 978-1-4525-8398-3 (e)

Library of Congress Control Number: 2013918191

Printed in the United States of America.

Balboa Press rev. date: 10/05/2013

BALBOA
PRESS
A DIVISION OF HAY HOUSE

Acknowledgements

A special thank you to my friend Susan Dunderdale Jones who has helped
me over recent years to understand and connect with the orbs.
Thank you to my beautiful family, who knows Mum has had another calling
when she dashes out into the garden again with camera in hand.
With enormous gratitude, I acknowledge the beautiful orbs and light anomalies for showing
up so much in my photographs. I love connecting with them all in this way. Namaste

Amazing Orbs

A wonderful journey of discovery

I have had all kinds of different light anomalies show up in my photos over the most recent years of my life and it has actually happened since the sad loss of my husband. Since then, I have been and still am on the most amazing and wonderful spiritual journey.

I would not class myself as different to anyone else but I do have this gift of connecting to the light energies that surround us on a daily basis, many having the most vibrant colours that shine with the most beautiful luminosity and it all happens in my photos.

There are books on the subject of orbs and these books offer good explanations but I am beginning to discover that they can have more profound meanings for each and every one of us. Do a lot of the orbs have messages, healing properties and do they help us at this moment in time on earth?

This first book is more of a picture book, as I want to share with you many of my amazing photos. I hope you see the immense beauty that these orbs carry too, I do see them backlit on a computer screen where they look absolutely stunning.

Connecting to the photos within this book you can experience the healing energies and transformational properties of all the pure and loving spiritual energies that surround us everyday.

Orbs do love appearing in family gatherings, happy occasions like weddings and anniversaries, parties, musical events in fact anywhere the energies are raised. They also appear well in damp conditions because they are energy and therefore are able to show up more easily. You can find them by the sea, waterfalls and of course when it is raining. I have also had magnificent flying orbs too, when you see the distance they have travelled in the time of a flash, they are travelling at the most amazing speed.

I take most of my photos with a Nikon automatic camera, which has 6 million mega pixels, which nowadays is much fewer than the new cameras on the market. When taking orb photos you mostly need to have the flash operating, or lately I find in bright sunshine they can use light reflections to manifest in.

All photos are genuinely from my camera, only three of the photos in this book have been just lightened to see them better. A lot of my photos are taken when dark, hence very dark backgrounds. When I have the opportunity I also love taking photos in places with high energies, like ancient stone circles. I personally do believe the orbs carry the energies of Angels, Spirits, Unicorns, Dolphins, Fairies and other high vibrations. I also sometimes see images quite clearly within the orbs.

Enjoy a journey of discovery into a world of luminosity, colour, shapes and geometric patterns. Begin your personal journey here, for me it has been and still is, a truly amazing journey of experiencing and transformation.

This group of orbs I find so
fascinating, some are travelling
very fast.

Looking like a group of orbs with truly vibrant colours.

4

Just like a firework display with fantastic colours.

This beautiful green orb appeared in my lounge.

A rainbow heart.

An amazing pattern within rings.

Pretty energy colours surround this orb.

My first orb which appeared in the kitchen. It radiates such beauty, colour and light.

Looking just like a flower.

This fast moving orb appeared by some sunflowers in the lounge.

A very different shaped orb with patterns within.

Looking just like a flying bird this orb
radiates amazing colour.

Turquoise, green, pink and purple are with this orb.

Not always round but this orb has some
beautiful green energy to see.

Very clear rings within and a fascinating pattern.

Another truly amazing orb.

Gold, turquoise, blue and purple
surround this delightful orb.

A different shape with lovely subtle colours.

A very fast flying orb with beautiful turquoise to the right.

Delightful energy colours.

The perfect circle with rings so clear.

A very fast flying colourful orb.

These two came from a photo of many orbs in my garden.

Looking like birds!

Blues through to greens at a speed.

A different looking pale brown orb with
very subtle patterns.

Colourful orbs which look like they are having a meeting!

Another unique orb.

An orb so different.

Such a textured orb.

This bright light has a huge blue energy to it.

A very pretty orb appeared by my rhododendron shrub, looks like a flower itself.

This orb appeared by a gong.

Looking just like a tropical flower.

Appearing on my patio, almost a domed honeycomb pattern.

Looks just like an owl flying.

Another garden orb.

Clear rings and a smooth look, taken
with a different camera.

A little one radiating so much purple energy.

To the left of the statue a ball of blue energy and in front one of the biggest and brightest flying orbs.

An interesting pattern within.

This orb appeared in a room whilst staying in Glastonbury.

Almost like a snowstorm.

Unusual shape and leaving a fast trail.

Pink and purple around with more
amazing patterns.

Taken at Avebury on a different camera.

I love the pink, purple and blue on this very bright orb.

Flying with amazing colour.

In my next book with Susan Dunderdale Jones it will include some of my personal story and why so many fairies have also appeared in my photos. We will also journey through the orbs, to discover the magic of the orbs where with guided meditation we will connect with the orbs in the photos and discover what happens - for us a truly amazing journey of experiencing, healing and transformation.

Lightning Source UK Ltd.
Milton Keynes UK
UKIC01n1955031113
220296UK00002B/18

9 781452 583976